D0385841

AMONG FRIENDS

BY
ROXIE KELLEY

ILLUSTRATIONS BY
SHELLY REEVES SMITH

Published by CRACOM Corporation
12131 Dorsett Road, Maryland Heights, Missouri 63043

ISBN 0-9633555-5-4

© 1994 by Among Friends
Printed in Canada

Art on page 22 was inspired by the floral design work of Gayle Bingham, Town & Country Flowers.

Last digit is the print number: 9 8 7 6 5 4 3 2 1

" *T*he proper business

of friendship is to

inspire life and courage;

and a soul thus supported

outdoes itself…"

- Joseph Addison

The best friendships are often formed when

you're busy thinking about something else.

With no

walls up and your

guard down

you're charmed by

someone's

unprotected

presence.

One pleasant moment leads to another…

one common thread is delicately

woven in and through and

around about…

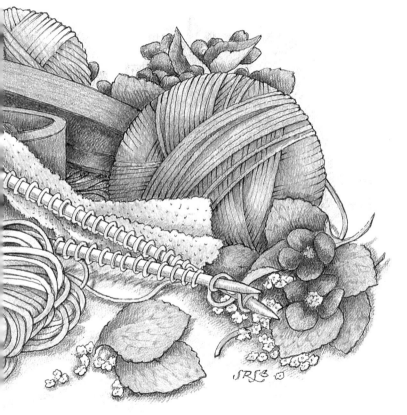

*U*ntil you feel so connected that you seem

to be speaking with one heart and one mind.

ou find yourself smiling
when they smile,
hurting when they hurt.

*D*reaming

and scheming

with them,

*H*oping

and

coping

*T*iming becomes a

respected piece of this

friendship puzzle

as you think

about how and why

and when you met...

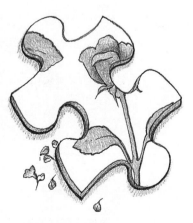

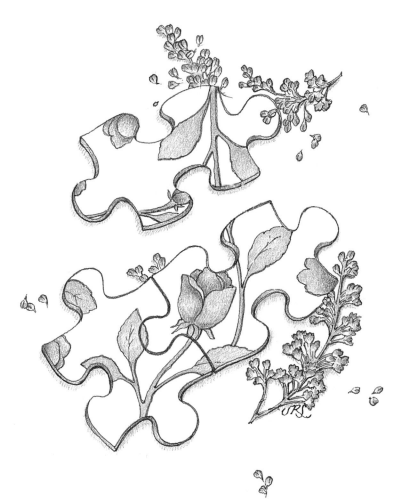

nd one day

you become

aware of

the importance

of this presence

in your life...

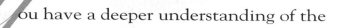

*Y*ou have a deeper understanding of the

words gratitude and growth,

and

*P*leasure

and peace.

Finally

it becomes clear

how precious

this one life

has become to yours.

And you know

you have been

graced

with the gift

of a friend.

A·M·O·N·G
FRIENDS